Just For

Mom

Adult Coloring Book

Coloring2Relax

Coloring2Relax Publishing

support@coloring2relax.com

Printed in the United States of America

First Printing, 2017

http://www.coloring2relax.com

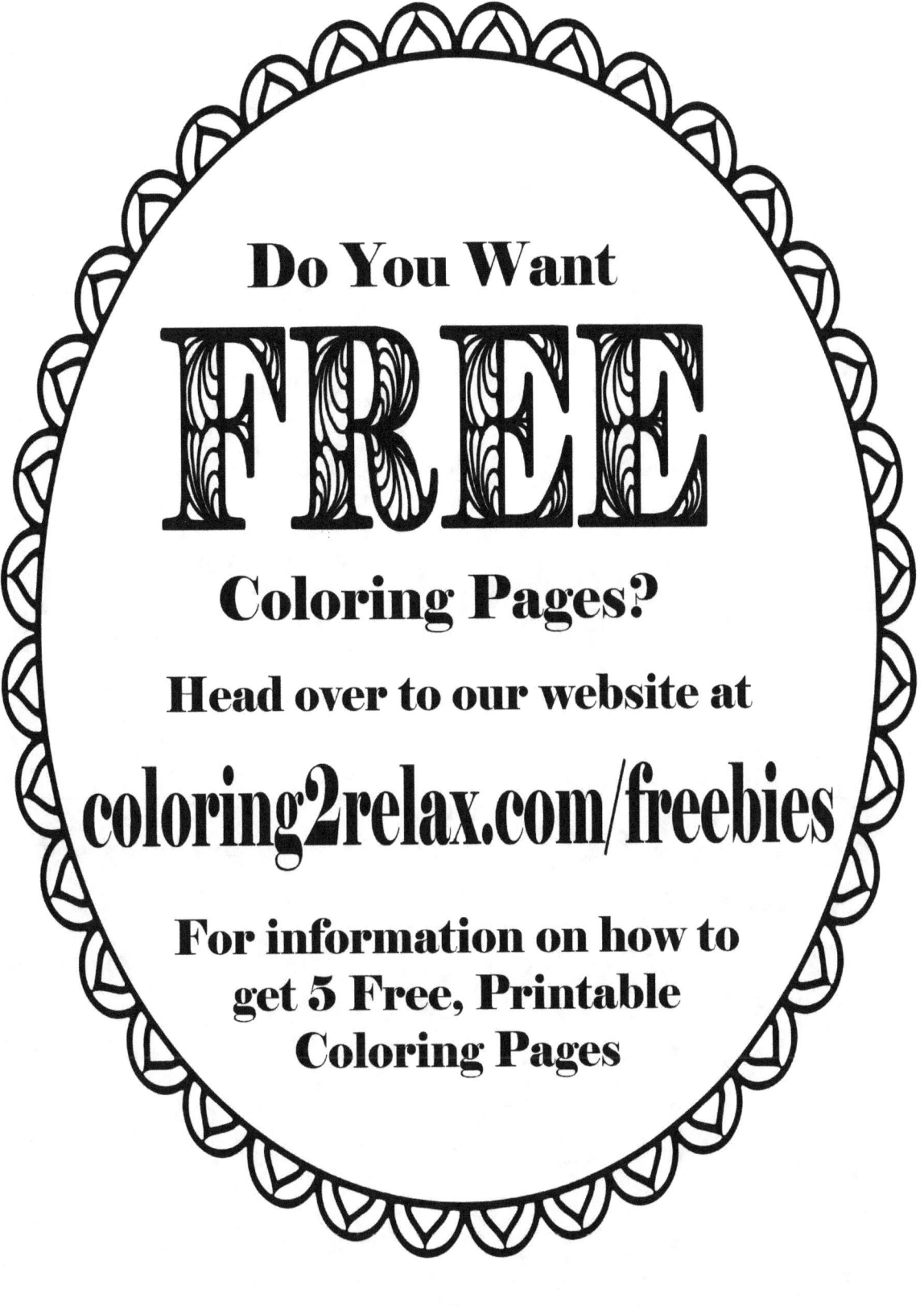

Do You Want

FREE

Coloring Pages?

Head over to our website at

coloring2relax.com/freebies

For information on how to get 5 Free, Printable Coloring Pages

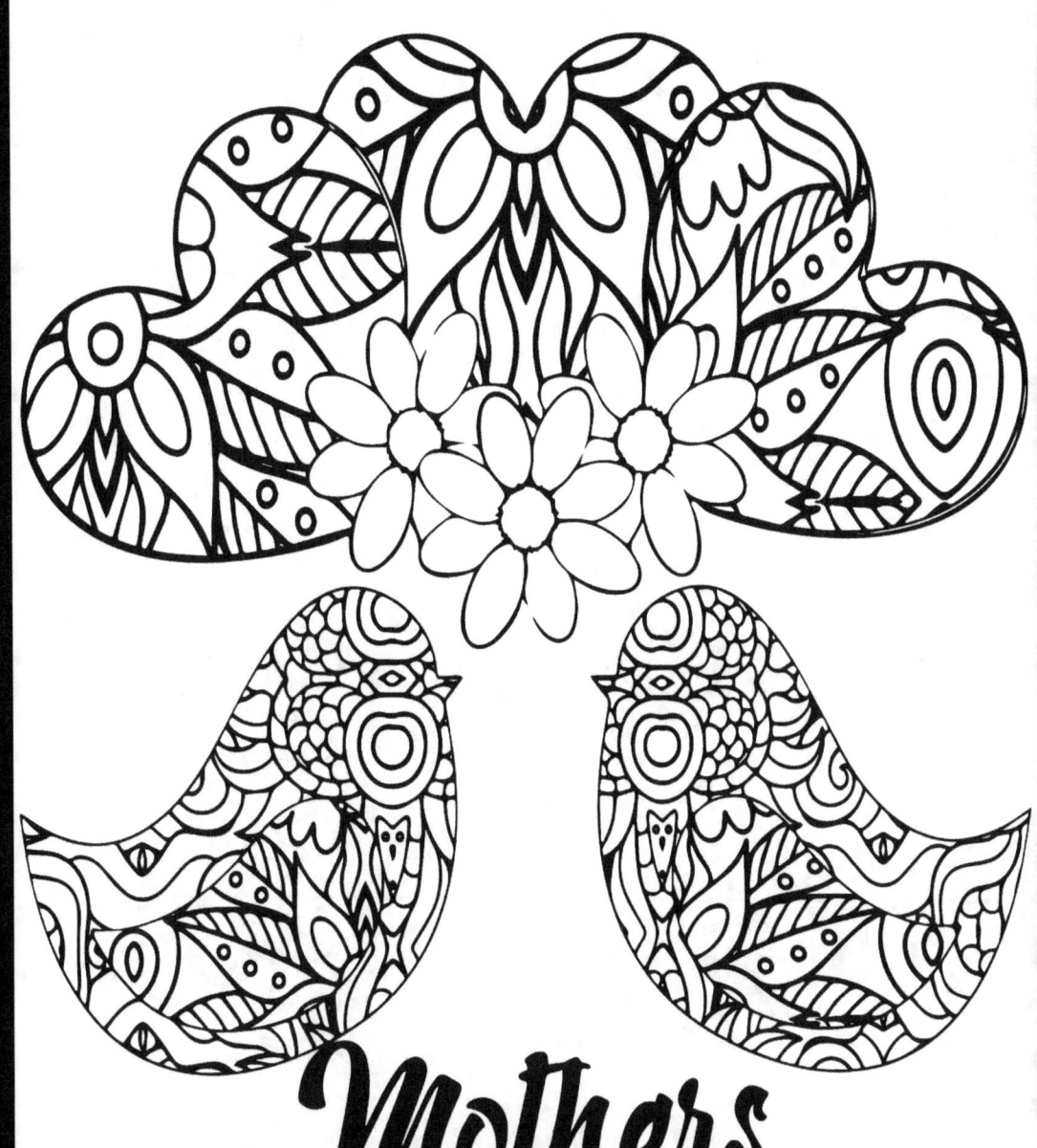

Always My Mother

Forever My Friend

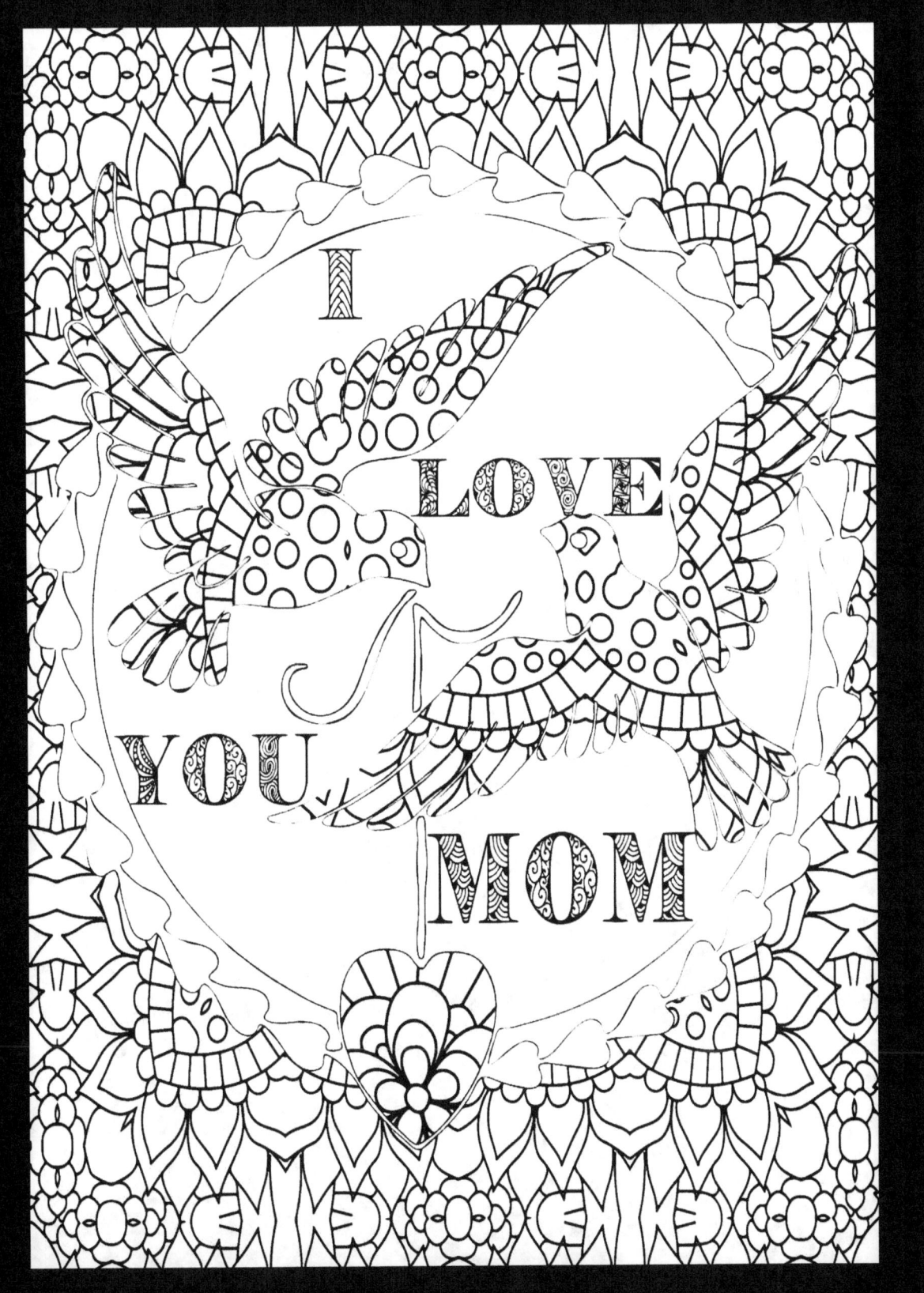

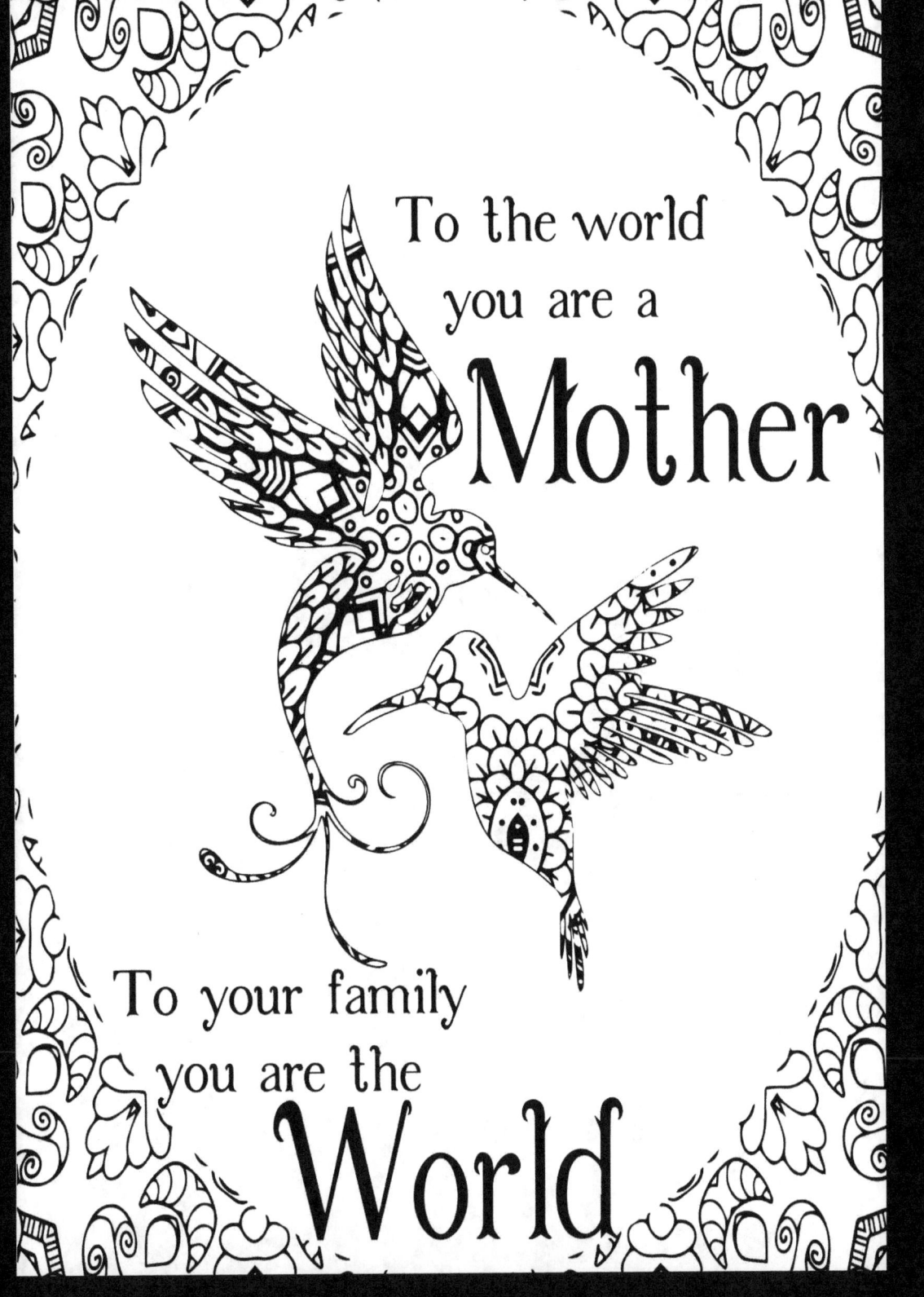

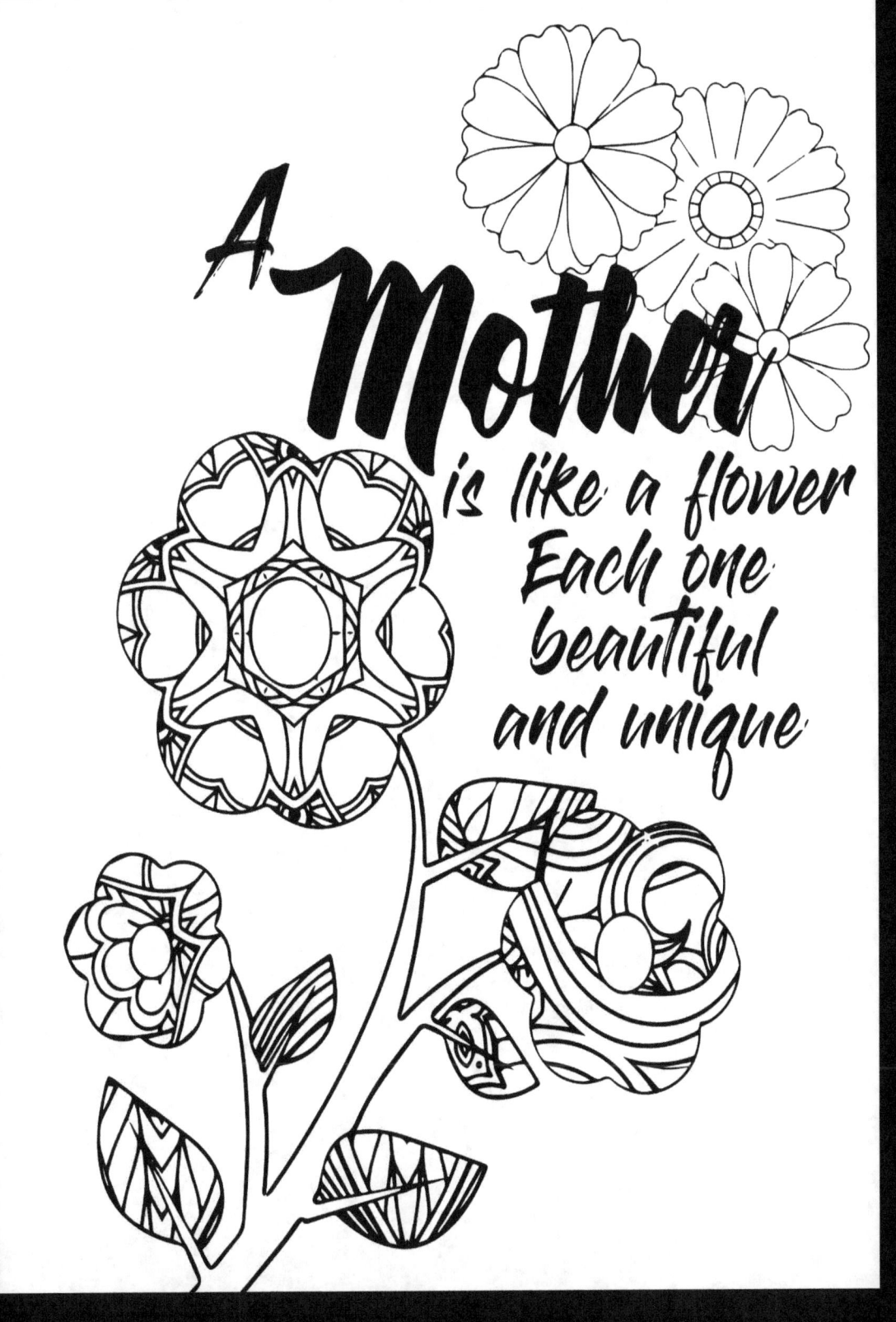

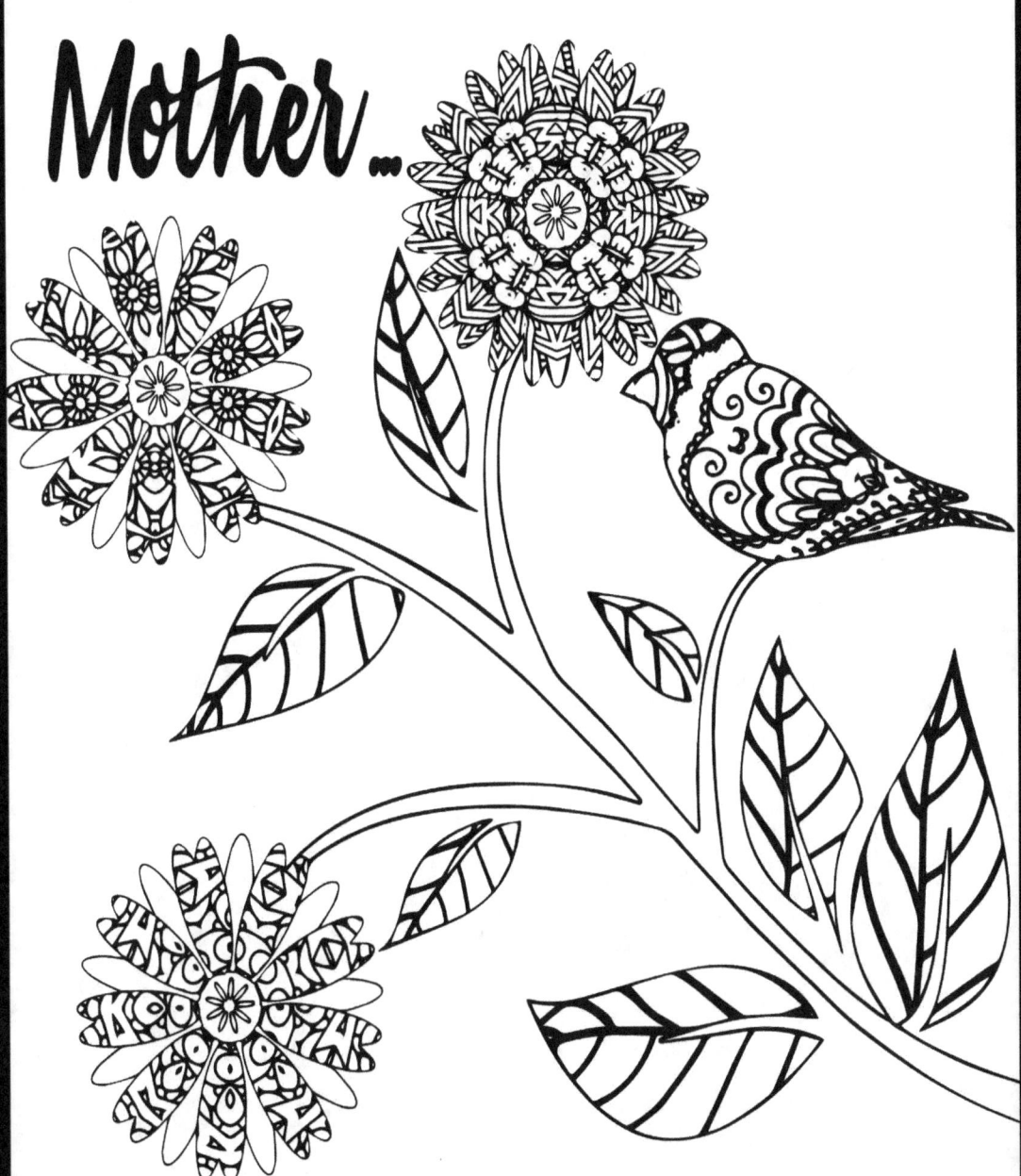

Mother...

Where life begins
and love never ends

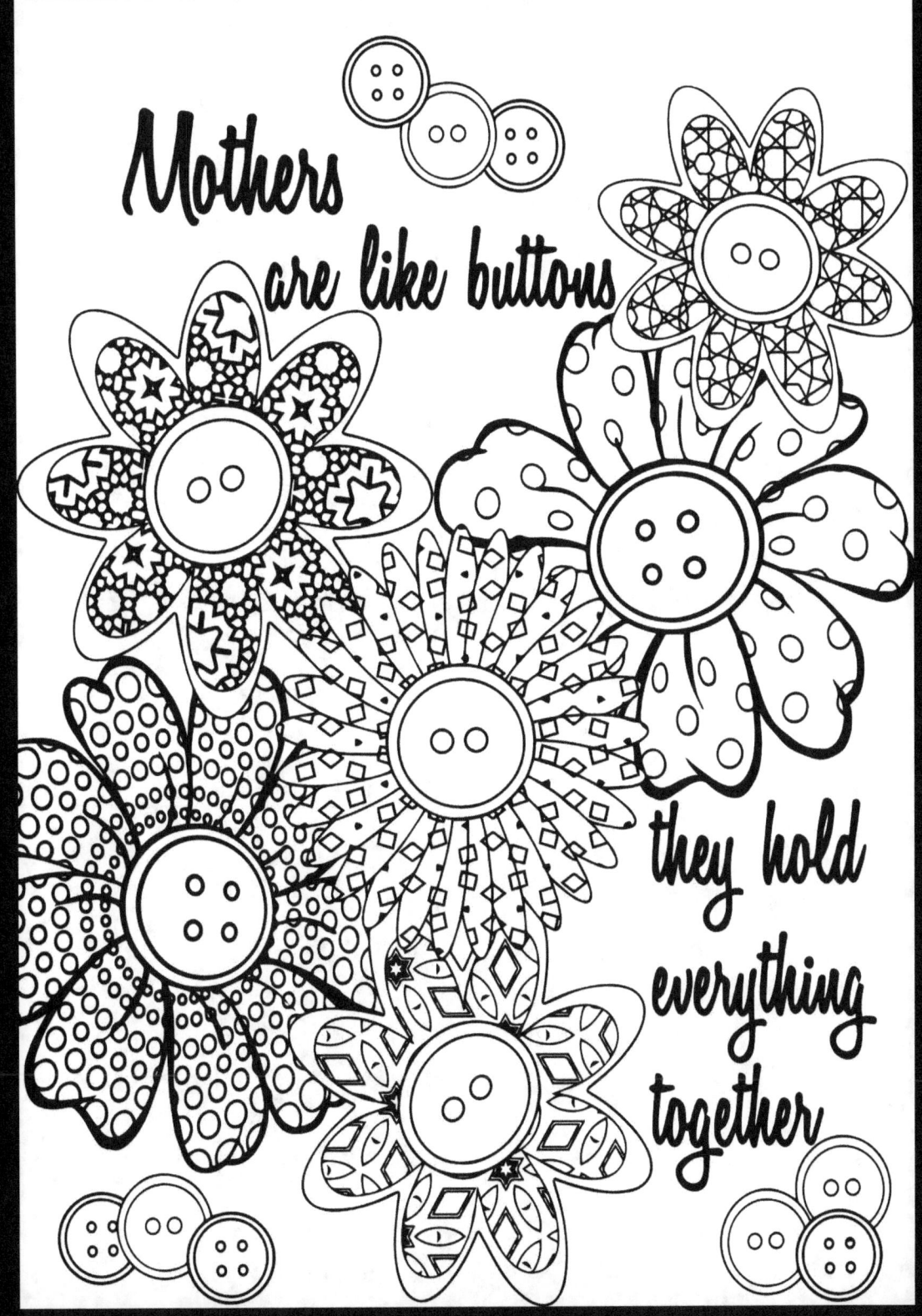

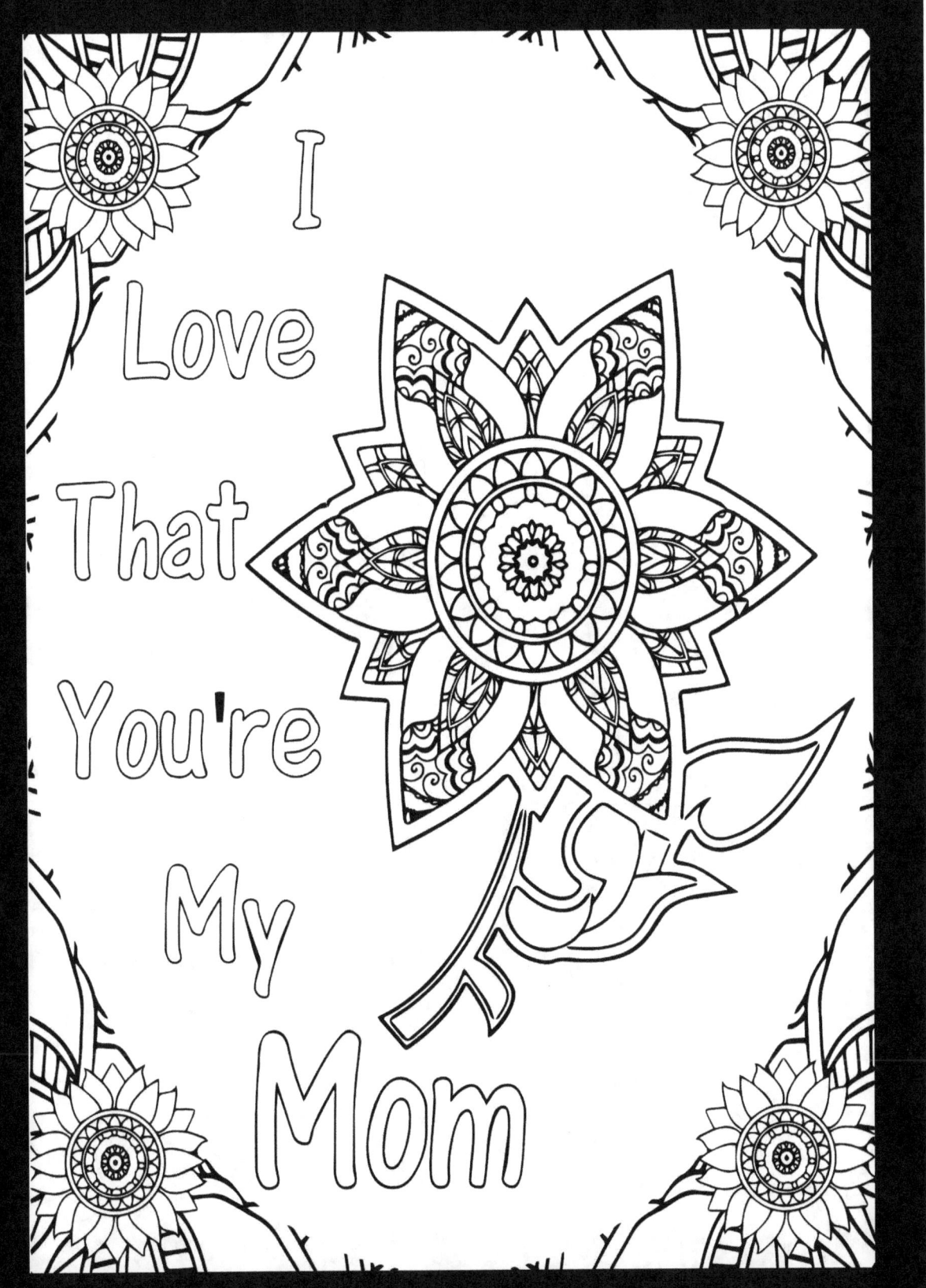

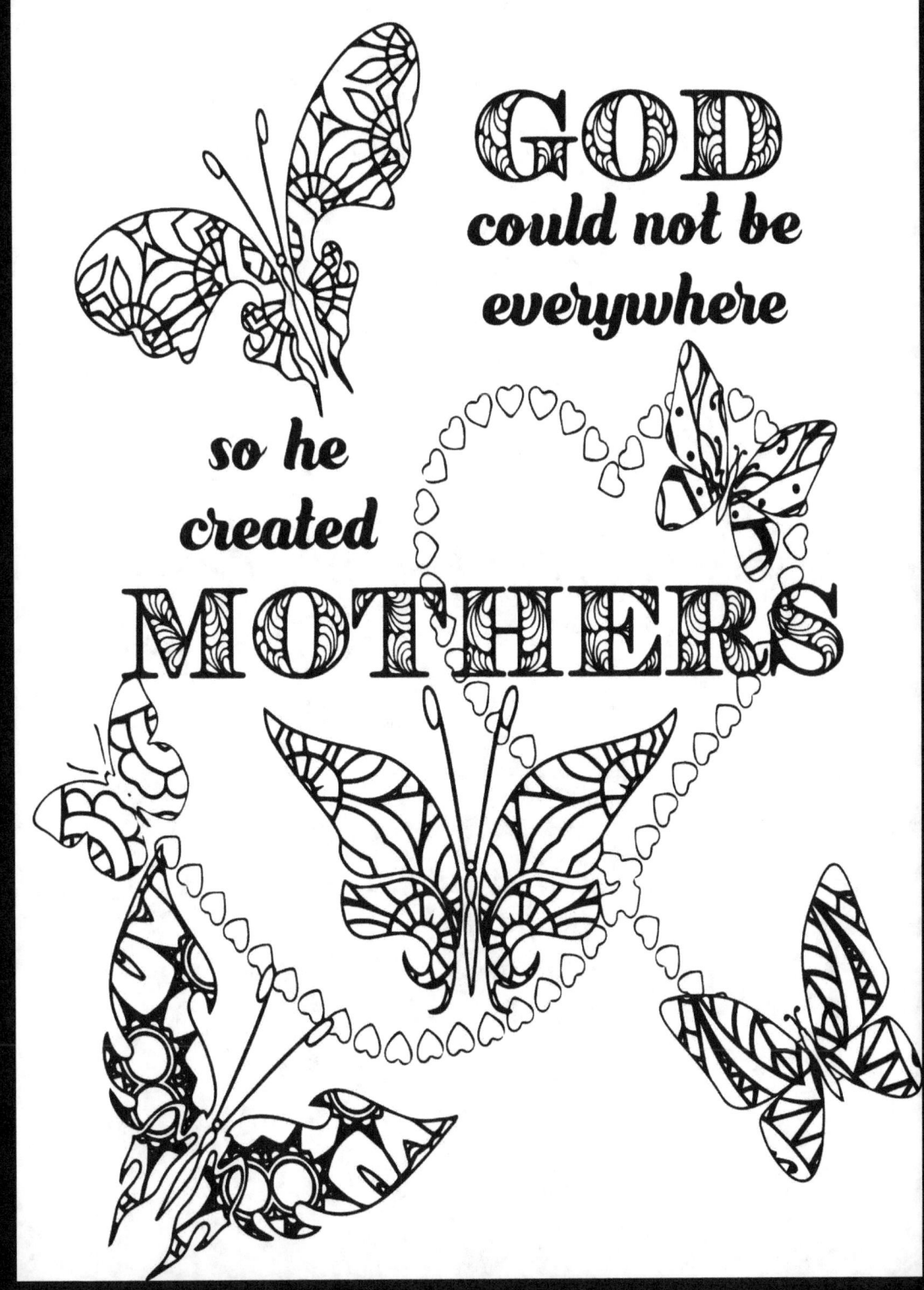

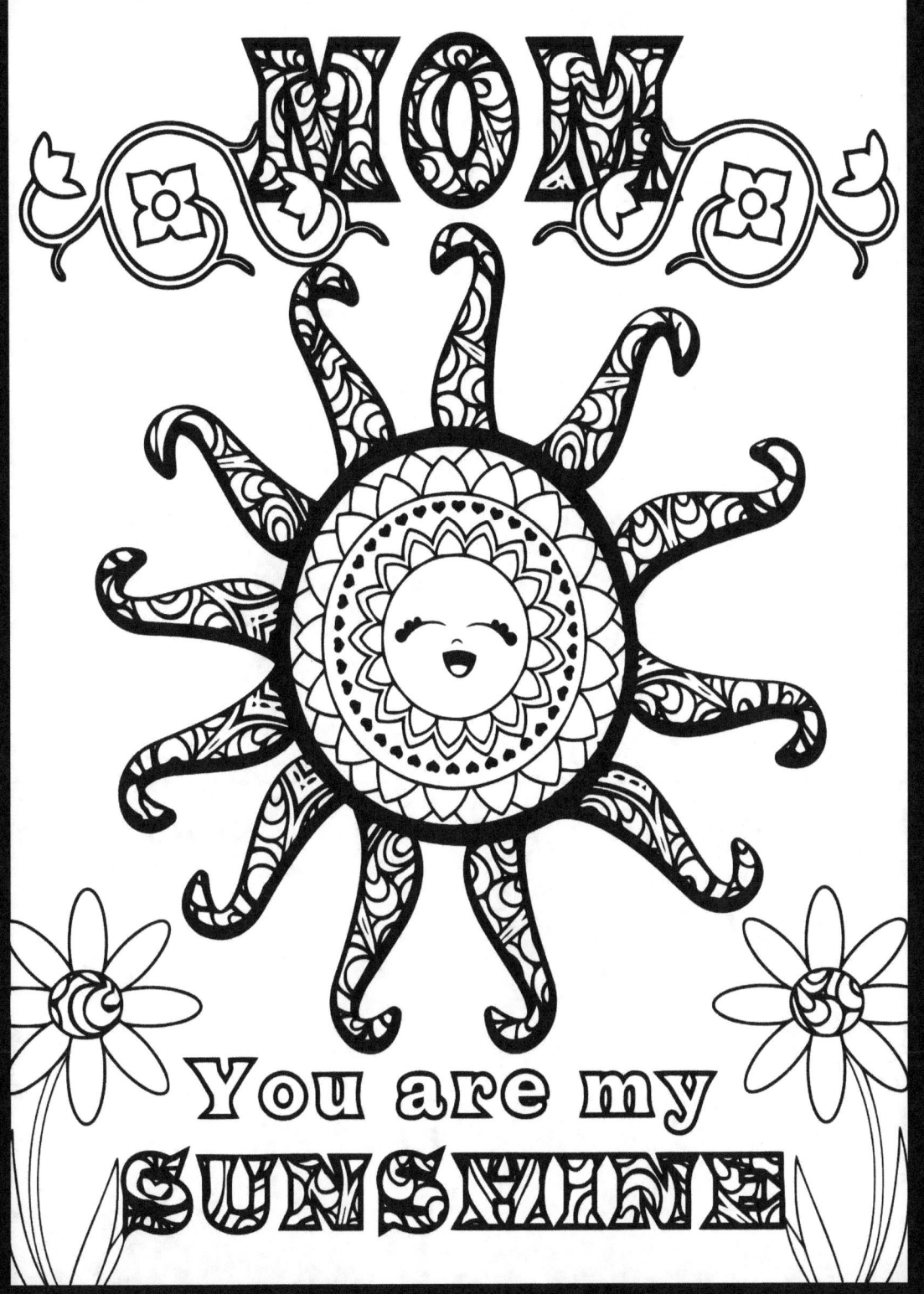

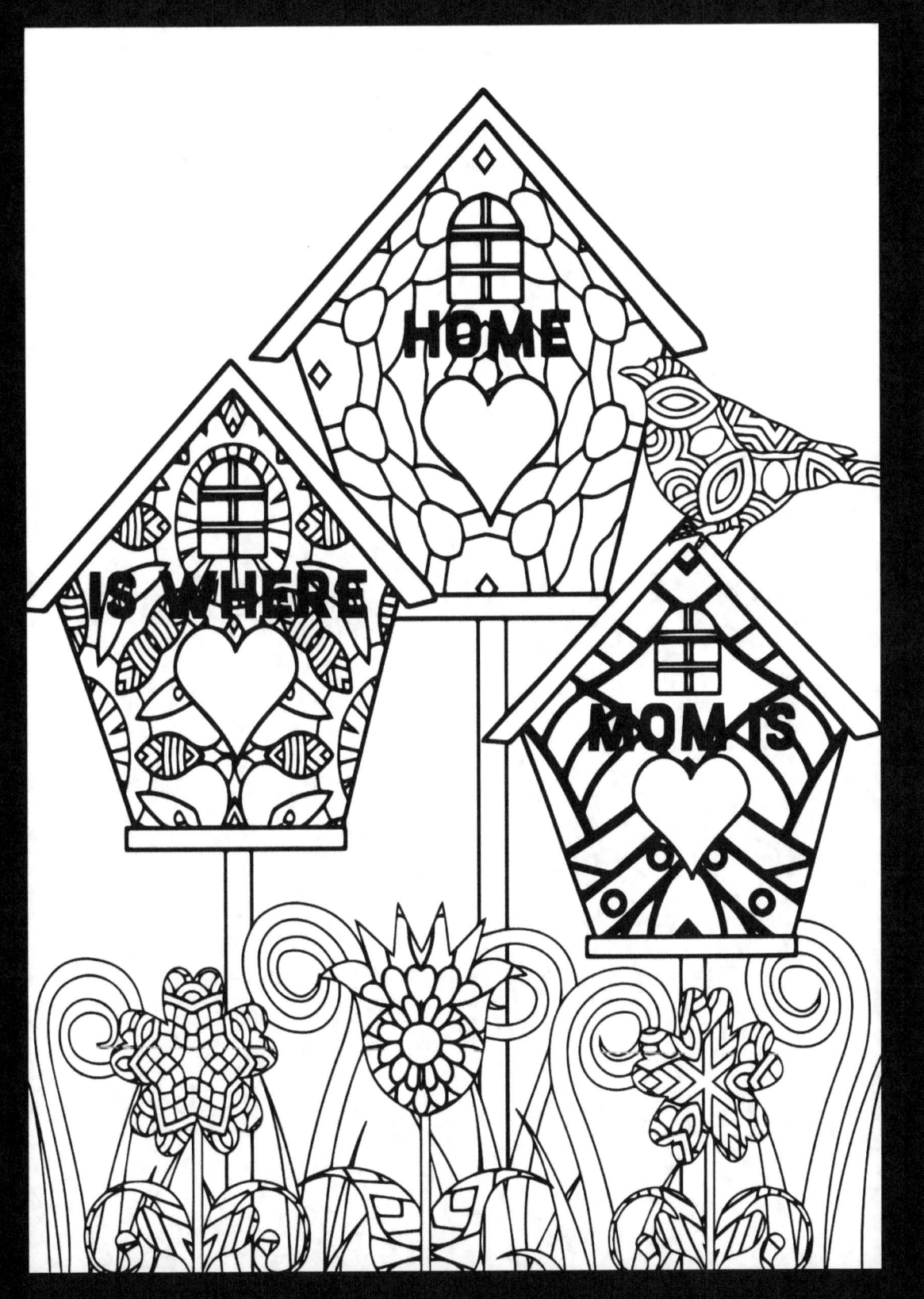

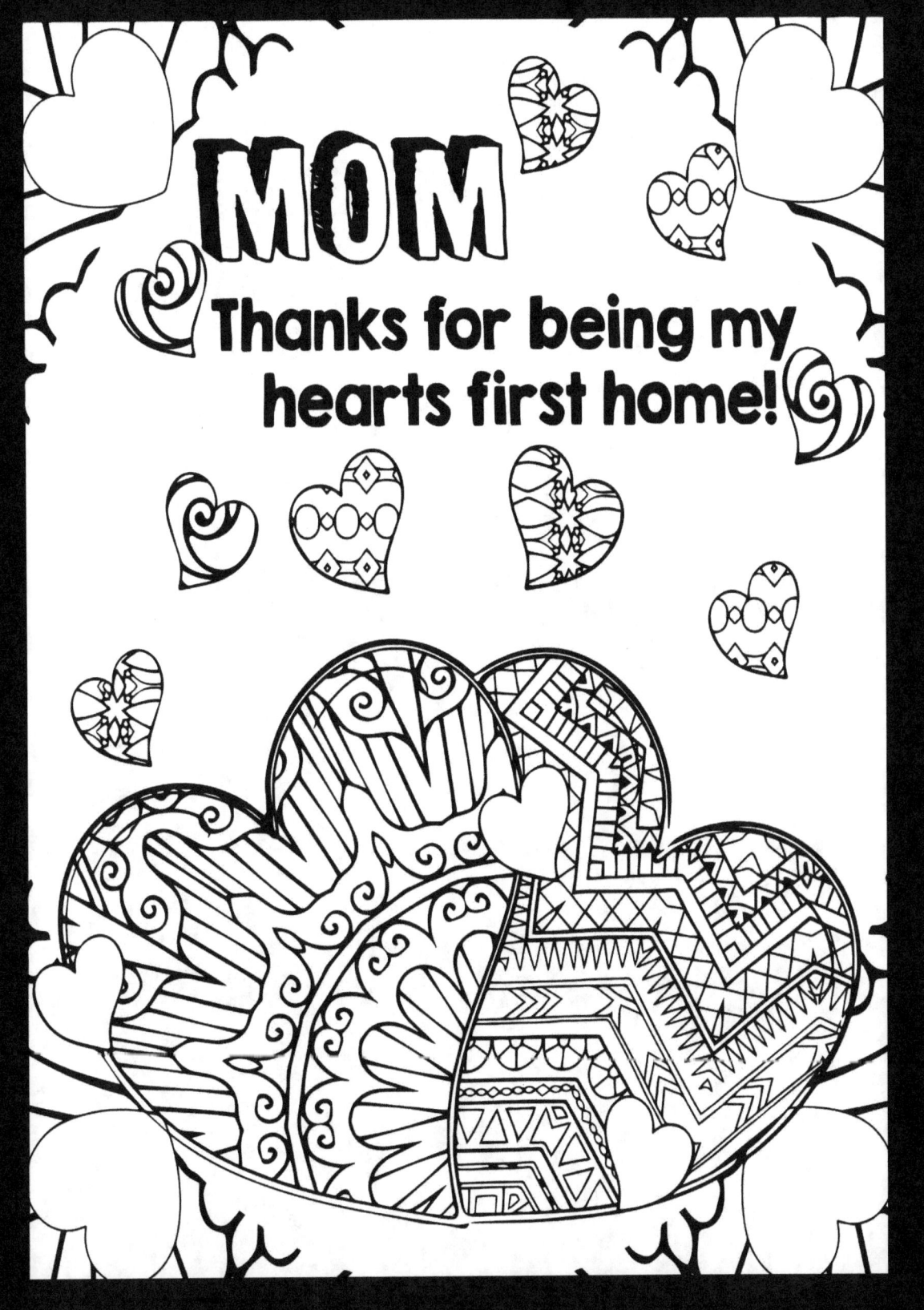

Of all the gifts that life has to offer . . .

Mother is the greatest of them all

Life doesnt come
with a manual...

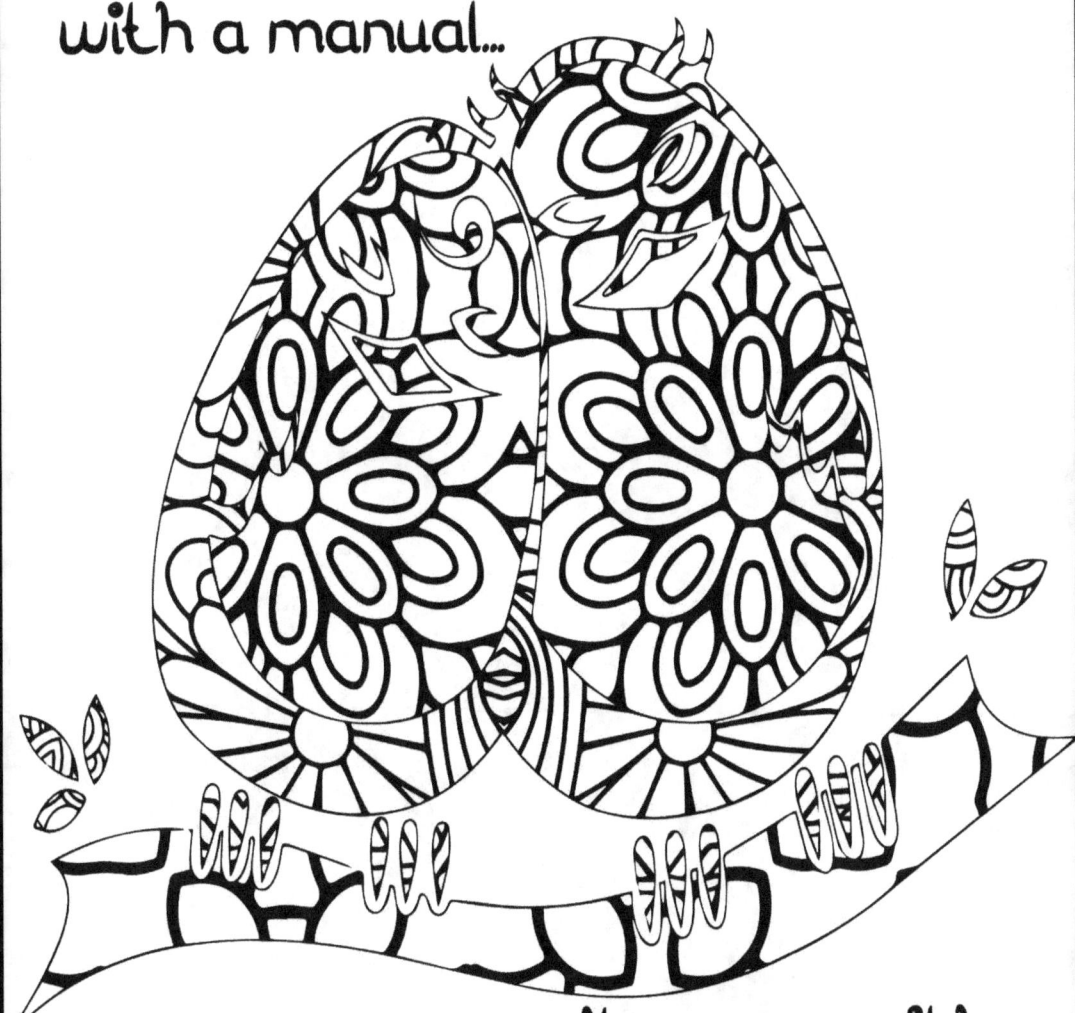

It comes with a

Mother

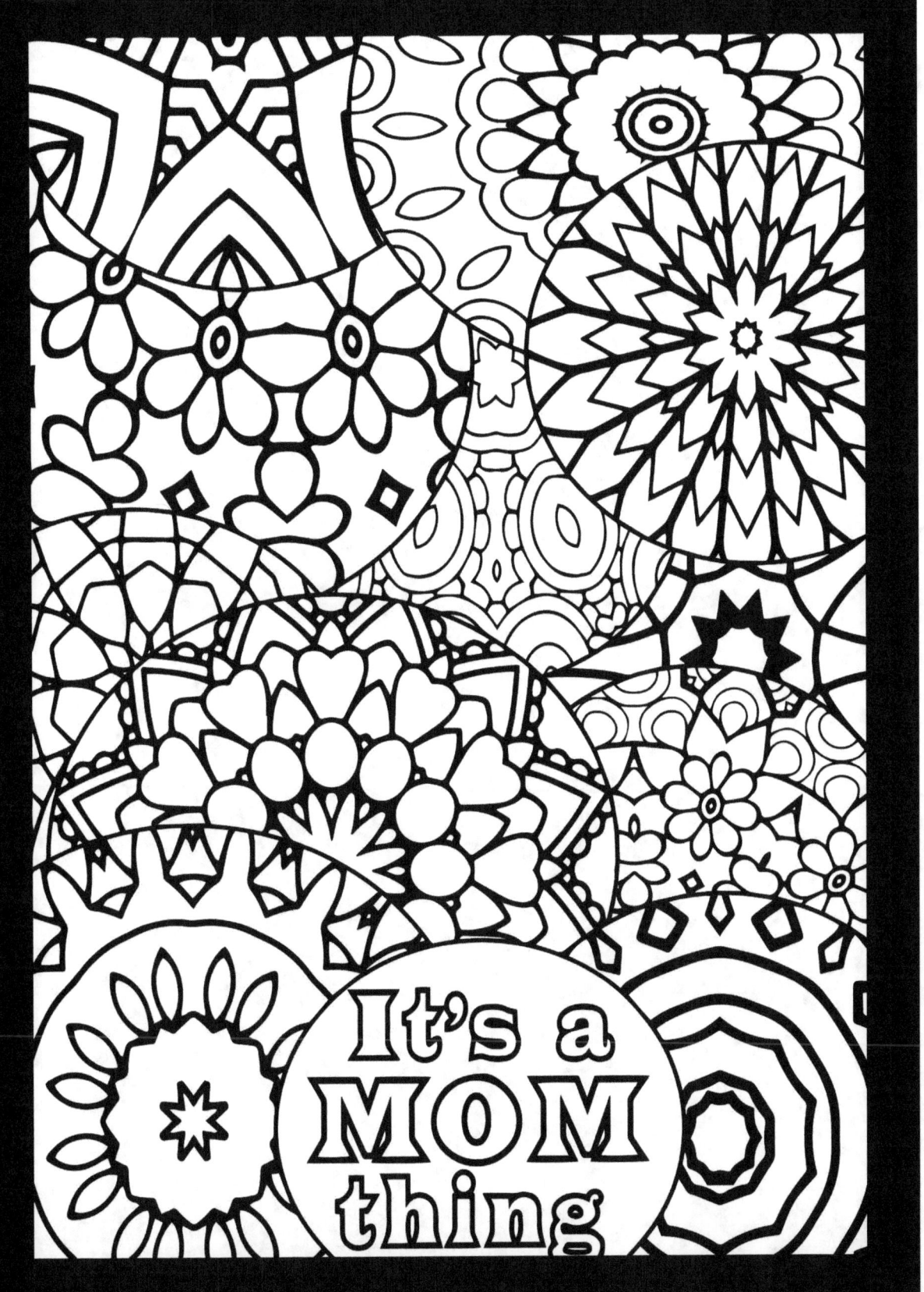

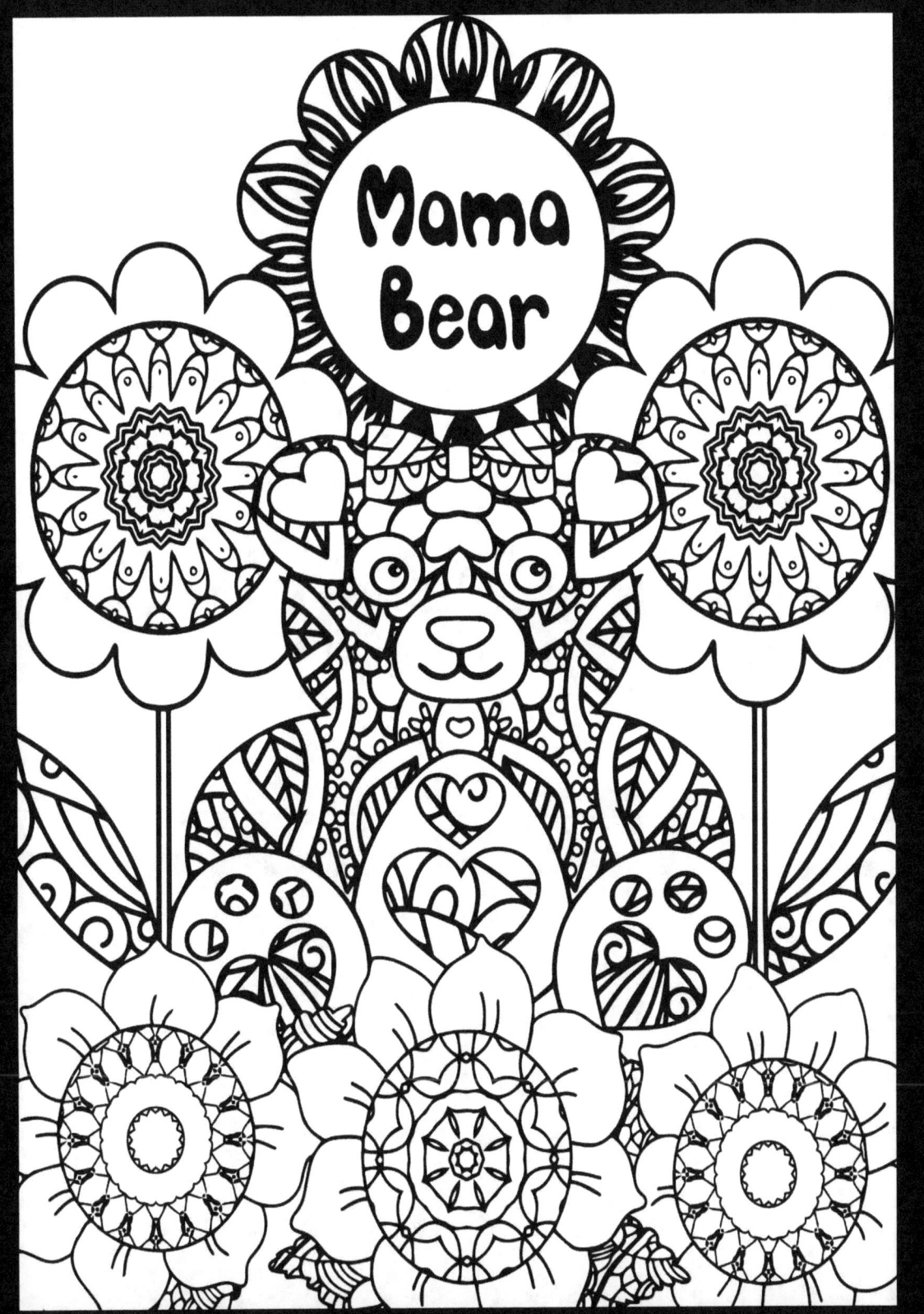

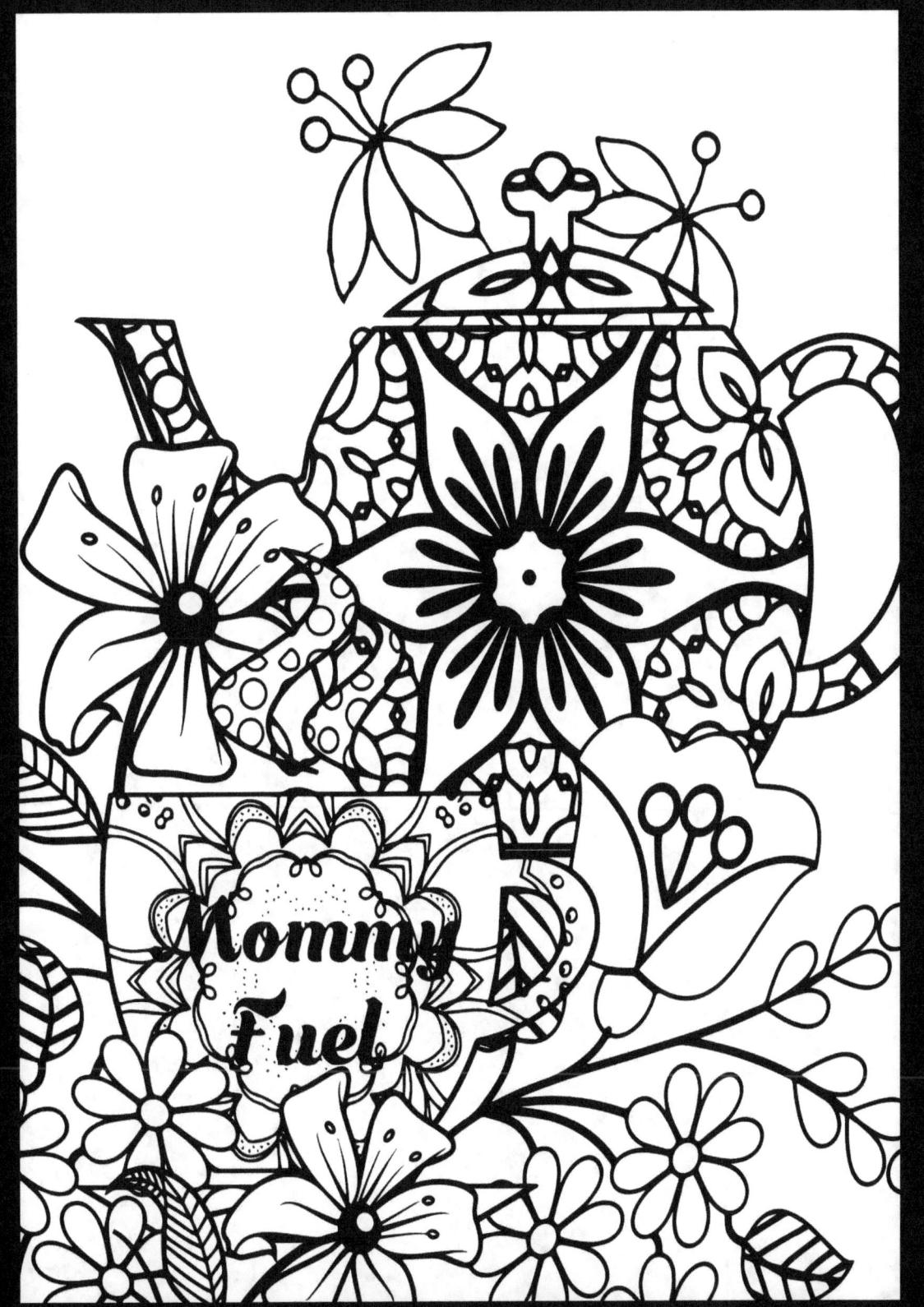

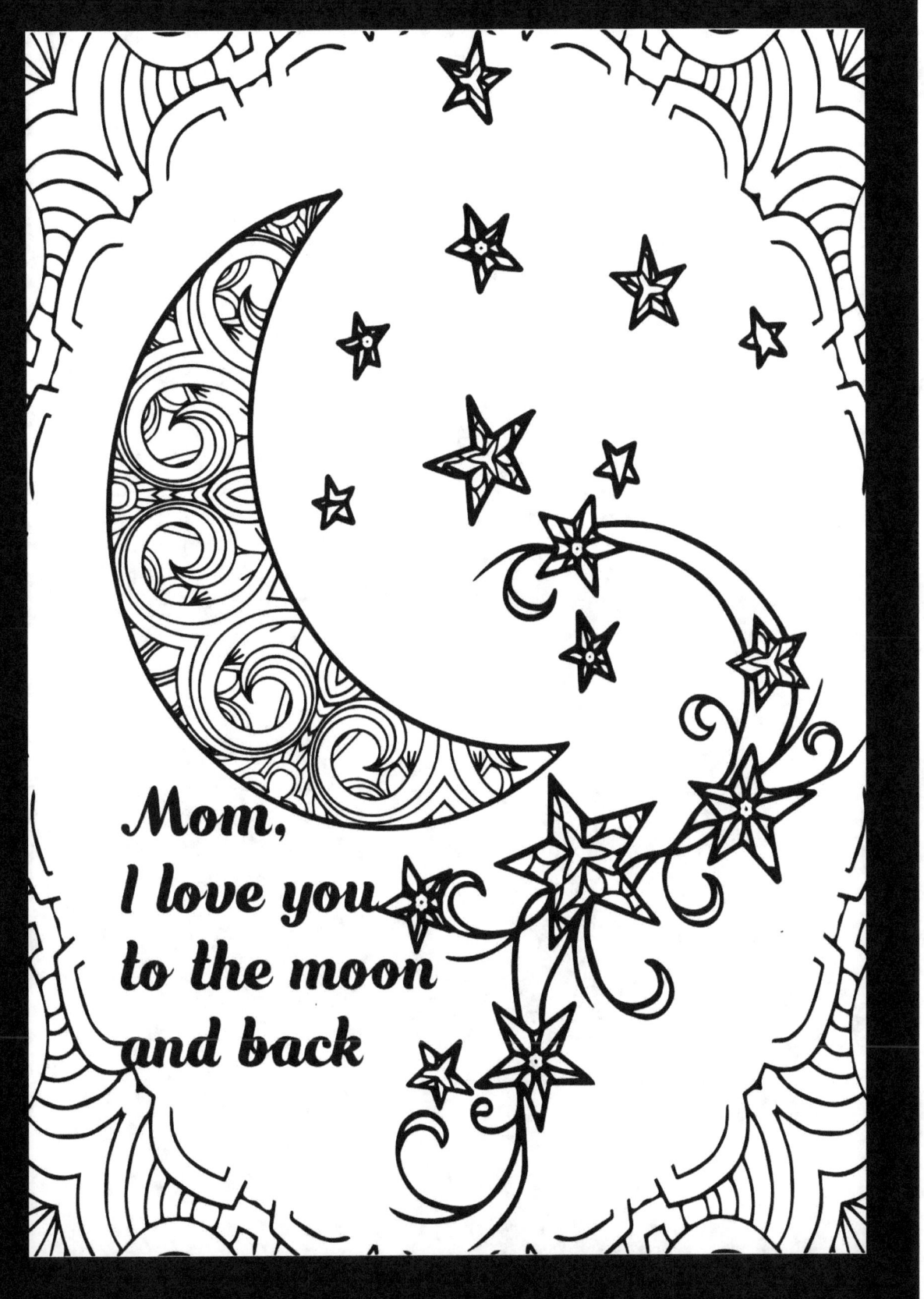

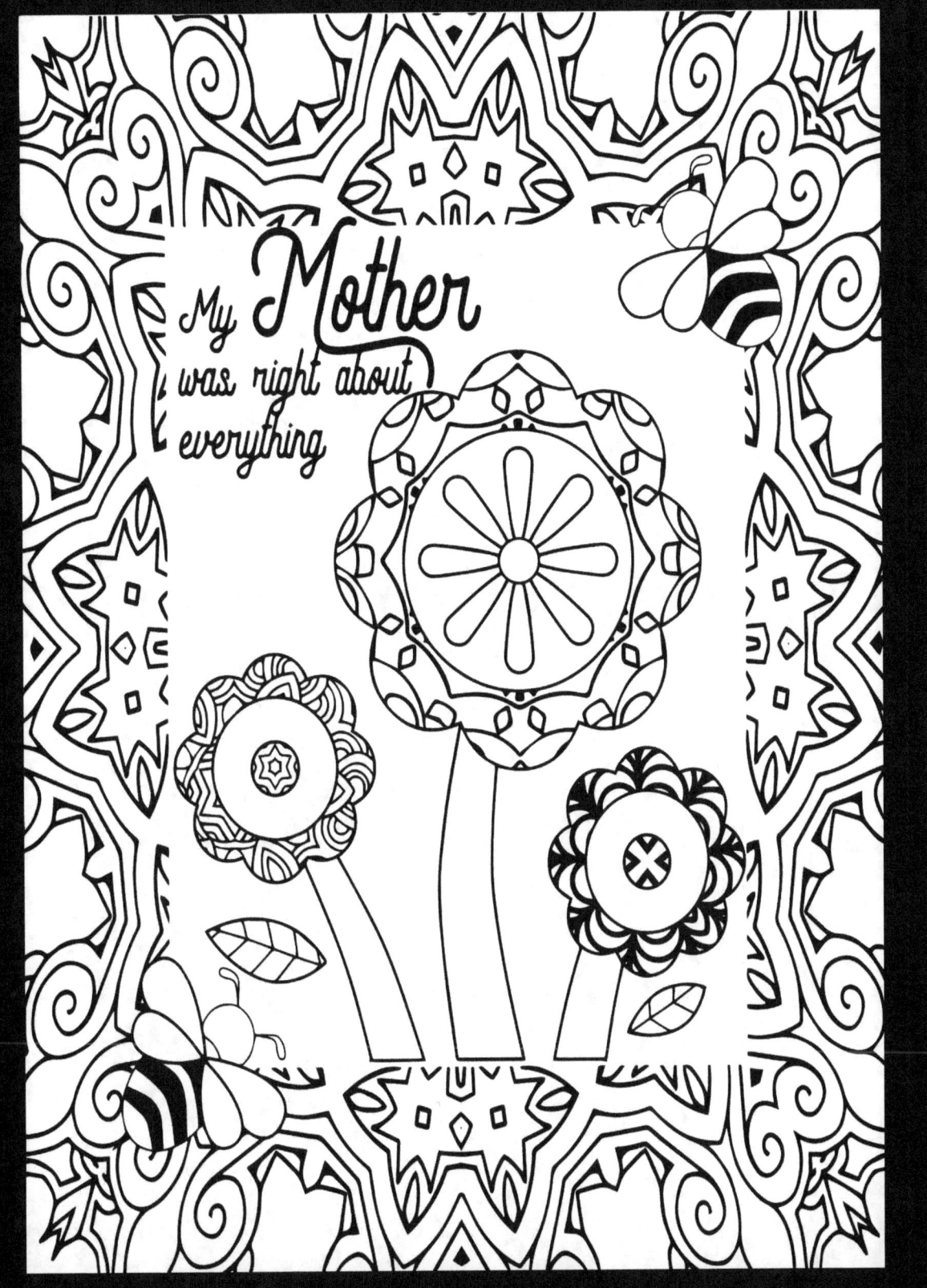

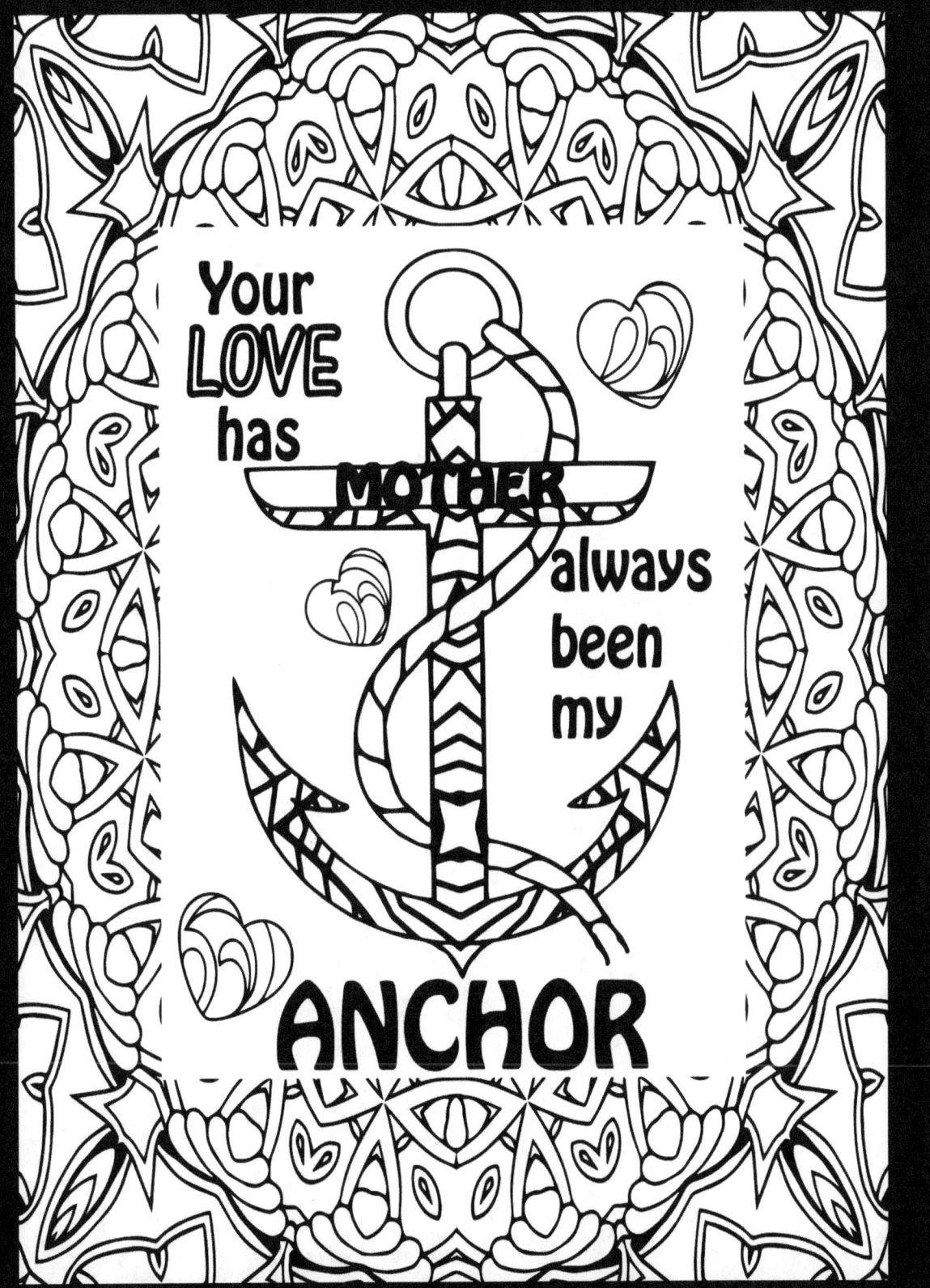

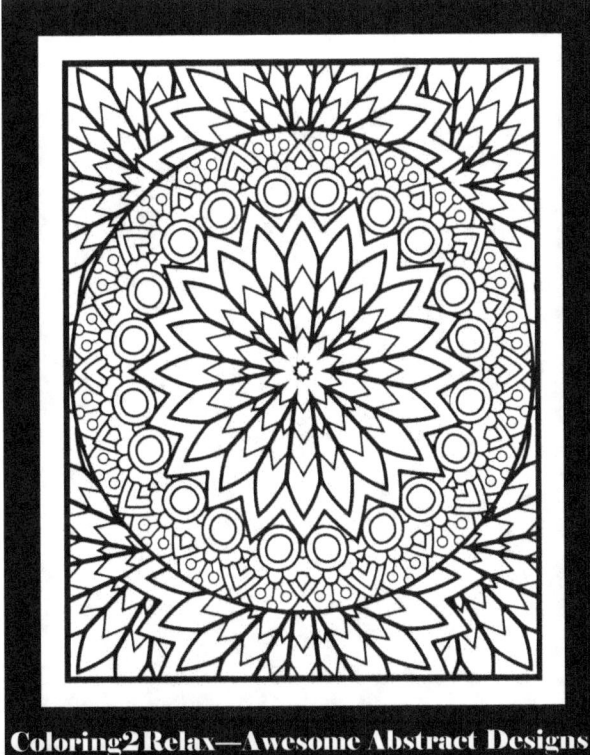

Coloring2Relax—Awesome Abstract Designs

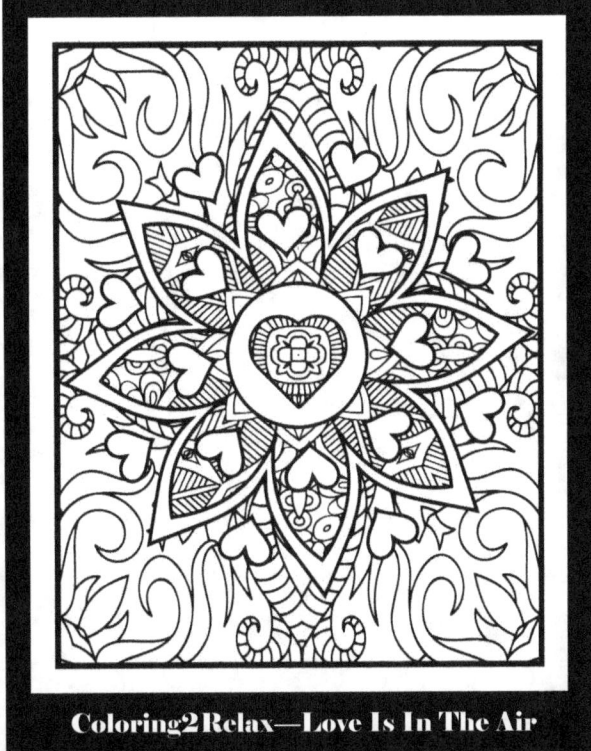

Coloring2Relax—Love Is In The Air

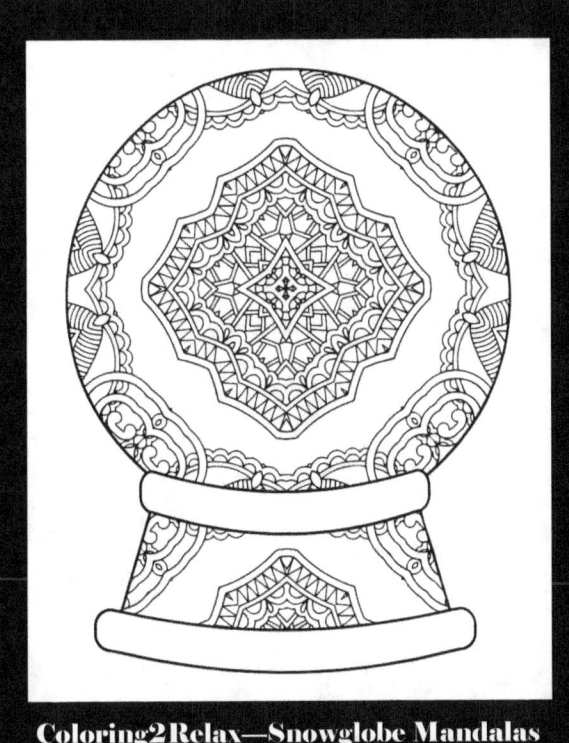

Coloring2Relax—Snowglobe Mandalas

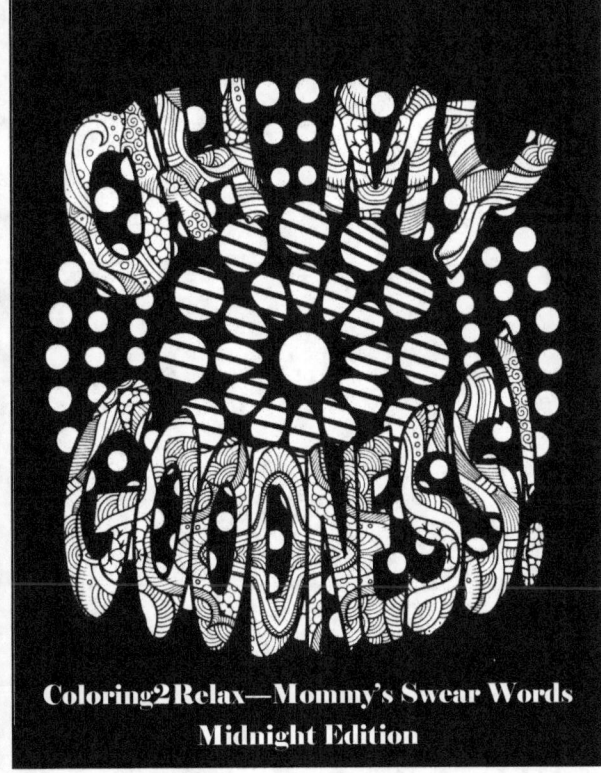

Coloring2Relax—Mommy's Swear Words Midnight Edition

Samples of Coloring Pages from some of our most popular Adult Coloring Books. Please visit our website, www.coloring2relax.com to shop more of our Adult Coloring Books and Journals. And don't forget your Freebies while you are there!

Coloring Practice Page

Practice blending & Shading, try new colors, test markers & gel pens,
decide on color palettes or add color palettes you want to use later

Coloring Practice Page

Practice blending & Shading, try new colors, test markers & gel pens,
decide on color palettes or add color palettes you want to use later

Coloring Practice Page

Practice blending & Shading, try new colors, test markers & gel pens,
decide on color palettes or add color palettes you want to use later

Coloring Practice Page

Practice blending & Shading, try new colors, test markers & gel pens,
decide on color palettes or add color palettes you want to use later

Coloring Practice Page

Practice blending & Shading, try new colors, test markers & gel pens,
decide on color palettes or add color palettes you want to use later

Coloring Practice Page

Practice blending & Shading, try new colors, test markers & gel pens,
decide on color palettes or add color palettes you want to use later

Blank Page

Pull out and use under the page you are coloring for added protection against bleed through and denting.

Blank Page

Pull out and use under the page you are coloring for added protection against bleed through and denting.

Blank Page

Pull out and use under the page you are coloring for added protection against bleed through and denting.

Blank Page

Pull out and use under the page you are coloring for added protection against bleed through and denting.